ENTHUSIASTIC ENDORSEMENTS FOR

Sales Secrets of a Telemarketing Queen.

Mary Shanley has mastered her game. Her brilliance shines through in this roadmap to high level sales success. It's simply a must read if you are serious about sales.

Gary Chappell
CEO
Nightingale Conant

"The world of telemarketing is populated by characters who over promise and under deliver. For 29 years, Mary Shanley and her family of telemarketing companies have stood head and shoulders above that crowd, providing a broad range of clients with innovative ideas, meaningful results, and plain old responsive service. I highly recommend that the reader listen and learn when they read Sales Secrets of a Telemarketing Queen."

Matt Crisci
President, CEO MGC Consulting
Who's Who in American Business, 1996 - 2012

"Mary Shanley's drive and persistence brought her sales team to the top of our numbers, the best outside team we've ever used at Business Breakthroughs and would happily use again. Mary knows sales and knows what works! -

Mitch Russo - President & CEO
Business Breakthroughs International
www.BusinessBreakthroughs.com
A Tony Robbins and Chet Holmes Company

Discovering Mary was one of those strokes of luck that on the surface doesn't appear to be meaningful at the time. Wasn't until I've had a long history of engagement with others in her industry that I could really appreciate her. Mary is in a class of her own.
Richard Capezzali,
EVP Kaplan university
SVP Education Dynamics
President and founder of Eduction Dynamics

For more information contact Mary Shanley at
maryshanley@callttc.com

Sales Secrets of a Telemarketing Queen!

A Quick easy-to-follow sales training
workbook with
Fool proof tips and cutting-edge
techniques that
ensure sales success.

Introduction

Welcome...and thank you for purchasing **Sales Secrets of a telemarketing queen.** I know that there are literally thousands of books that have been written about selling and the sales process, so I appreciate the fact that you've selected my book.

And I'm going to express that appreciation the best way I know how: by giving you a simple step-by-step process that will transform your sales profits from fair to good, from good to excellent, and from excellent to meeting all of your biggest dreams and financial goals in the shortest time possible.

Let's get started with a key point.

Selling is a simple process

How is it that some people are always closing deals? You know the folks I mean. They're like comic book action heroes...super-salespeople who can soar when the economy is crashing...fly high when everyone else seems to be crashing to earth. They make it look easy.

And you know what? It *is* easy...if you know how.

After nearly three decades in the world of business, I know how. I have trained and employed nearly 15,000 people in my telemarketing business through the years. The successful sales processes I developed to help my business thrive and grow are exactly what I've laid out in this guide.

I am going to show you how to take advantage of the telemarketing training we developed over the past 25 that were used to teach college students, part-time moms and even people who couldn't sell lemonade on the corner, how to sell just about anything.

Imagine what you can do with this information! These simple yet incredibly effective techniques, are going to show you how to become the most efficient, productive sales person that you can possibly become.

Sales Is A Win-Win Game

Do you think of sales as an adversarial relationship where you try to 'best' a potential buyer and bend him or her to your will so that you can extract money for your own profit? If you do -- and many people think of the sales process in exactly this way – I'm here to set you straight:

The relationship between buyer and seller is *mutually* beneficial.

A buyer has a need (or desire) that a seller can satisfy. When the deal is right, everybody wins.

I'd like to take a moment to talk about philosophy…mine…about selling and telemarketing.

I believe in doing business in an honourable way. At its heart, I believe that commerce is a two-way street where each party has a need that the other can satisfy. I believe in offering a good product at a fair price. All the tips, tactics, and strategies in this guide are based on the premise that you're an honest businessperson just like me. You are not trying to take advantage of anyone. You believe in your product or service and know that it will make your customers happier in their lives or more productive in their business.

As for telemarketing, I know a lot of people equate telemarketing with phone calls during the dinner hour.

Telemarketing is so much more than that. It's the friendly phone call from your dentist reminding you that it's time to set an appointment. It's the call from your bank that there are lower cost options on your checking account. It's the reduced pricing offer on a product you wanted to buy. It's a great way to have direct one-on-one with your customers; to hear the good and to hear the bad direct from your prospects and customers. It's an incredibly valuable sales and marketing option that almost every business uses in some way.

That's my philosophy on telemarketing and selling, and the psychology of each is closely related to it. As someone with a product or service to sell, your first question is, "Who am I selling to and what do I have to offer them that they can't get anywhere else?" The psychology part, the essence of selling, is

"How can I identify the needs of a prospect at the exact point when they are ready to make a purchase and determine how my product or service can best benefit them?"

Answering that question is what this guide is all about

You Can Do It!
As the saying goes, selling isn't rocket science. And while many people do, in fact, get formal training in sales at institutions of higher learning, many of the world's greatest dealmakers and salespeople have never even finished college. They got their education at another institution: The School of Personal Experience. And I'm going to share my experience to help you get to the head of the class, quickly.

The most important lesson any person involved in sales needs to master and which you may as well learn right here, right now is that

SUPER TIP # 1   Successful salespeople do the basics day in and day out without fail.

Successful salespeople are busy people. So they don't have time for complicated approaches to generating leads and closing sales. But no matter how busy they are, truly successful salespeople do <u>what needs to be done every day</u> and they <u>consistently bring in more new business</u> than the competition because of their actions. That's the 1st secret of successful telemarketing, doing the effective right actions-- time and time and time again.

.

Who This Book Is For

This book is for Y-O-U...whoever you are. It doesn't matter what business you are in. You can own an independent insurance agency or a day spa, a bank or be a Financial Advisor. You can be selling copiers, professional services or Printing. It doesn't matter who your customers are. You can be selling to soccer moms or plastic surgeons. It doesn't matter what the size of your business is or whether you're just starting out or firmly established.

If you follow these simple steps, you stand a good chance – a GREAT chance, actually – of leaving your competitors in the dust.

You see, more often than not, the business that effectively and consistently delivers its sales message is the one that <u>captures the lion's share of the profits</u>. This is precisely why a standardized approach to selling makes so much sense, no matter how large or small the company may be.

If you're in health care, insurance, retail, or any other area of business where <u>making a sale means making a profit</u>... the strategies in this book will work for you. And I urge you to **put them into practice as quickly as possible.**

A Sneak Peek at Your Journey and Destination

This Workbook is broken down into **9 Tactical Considerations** where you must compete to develop your selling routine. I've devoted a chapter to each consideration along with the 'Rules of the Game' and some tips from my personal playbook that will help you come out a winner:

Arena #1	**Product Knowledge**
Arena #2	**Customer Focus**
Arena #3	**Competition**
Arena #4	**Goals**
Arena #5	**Preparation**
Arena #6	**Selling Activity**
Arena #7	**Networking**
Arena #8	**Relationship-Building**
Arena #9	**Branding and Positioning**

Knowledge is power! So get ready to get going and improve your sales by

- **Knowing Your Product** – Understanding what makes your product or service a cut above the rest is the essence of your <u>sales advantage.</u> You need to be the expert in the field & be able to answer every question, quickly.

- **Knowing Your Customer** – Understanding who you are selling to and what is important to them drives your ability to <u>craft an irresistible message</u>

- **Knowing Your Competition** – Understanding who you are selling *against* allows you to make your offer more desirable and find the best niche to compete in.

- **Knowing Your Goals** – Understanding where you're heading in the short- and long-term helps you stay focused and on track and allows for continual measurement of where you are.

- **Knowing How To Prepare** – Understanding what is at the foundation of a successful sales transaction enables you to build a systematic approach you can use consistently

- **Knowing Your Selling RDA** – Understanding that selling is an ongoing activity helps you create daily processes that further your long-term sales goals. You understand what has to happen every single day to meet your goals.

- **Knowing Your Network** – Understanding that personal and professional contacts are the lifeblood of sales helps you build multiple streams of eager referrals

- **Knowing The Lifetime Value of A Customer** – Understanding that you can leverage your relationship with existing customers can help you sell more to customers you already have. There is always an opportunity to sell additional product or services to your customers.

- **Knowing The Meaning of Brand YOU** - Understanding exactly who you are and what you stand for allows you to establish an identity that stands out. And in this competitive world, you better have a really strong YOU brand that makes customers love & respect you.

Commit to the Small Steps that Lead to Big Profits
It's easy to get caught up in the race to outrun the competition and try to 100% better than 'the other guy.' But you know what? You don't have to be 100% better than your competition to win the business. You don't have to be 50% better.

**If you do just 1% better in your sales efforts than other businesses
in your niche, then you'll be the market leader!**

Small improvements lead to big profits. So commit to getting better...*a little better* in the 9 Tactical Arenas. Do whatever it takes to ensure that...

- Your familiarity with your product or service is just **1% deeper**

- Your knowledge of your target audience is just **1% more detailed**

- Your information-gathering is just **1% more thorough**

- Your goals are just **1% more well defined & specific**

- Your preparation is just **1% more comprehensive**

- Your processes are just **1% more systematic**

- Your business network is just **1% more extensive**

- Your relationship-building is just **1% more effective**

Everything you do should be focused on creating an environment that supports your sales efforts. You need to **frame your sales efforts** in ways that create bonds with your prospects and customers.

Replace ABC with ABO
In the David Mamet play/film 'Glengarry Glen Ross,' a group of real estate salespeople live by the code "ABC – Always Be Closing." Unfortunately, those who live by the code die by the code.

Rather than ABC, I believe in ABO – Always Be Opening. By that I mean you should always be opening doors, inviting people in, making them comfortable, and (here's the key) **listening to them.** Instead of thinking about making a sale, try and build a personal relationship with your prospect so you can better understand what their true needs are.

> **This is one of the most important techniques we taught our telemarketers. Listen to the customer. What are they telling you they need? Sell to their needs.**

When you talk to someone about your business, you need to be direct, authentic, and unattached to the outcome. When you stop selling and start listening and offering genuine solutions to problems, you will be viewed as a trusted resource instead of someone with only a sales agenda.

Wouldn't *you* rather buy from someone you trust? So would your prospect.

Tactical Arena #1 – Superior Product Knowledge

In the previous section, I dusted off the old (but true) chestnut that "Knowledge is power." Well, there's something else you need to understand about knowledge

Knowledge equals Confidence

If you want to fire up your enthusiasm in order to sell more, **find out all you can about your product, service, cause, or company.** The more you know about your product, the easier it is for you to identify the true benefits that will fire up your prospect's enthusiasm for your product and their confidence in you. You have to remember in this day and age no one is spending money foolishly or quickly. Everyone is doing a lot of research to buy the best product value for the money. So people like to buy from experts.

Perhaps you've heard it said that true salespeople don't need to know their products; that sales skills will make up for any deficiencies they might have in product knowledge. Some people are of the opinion that technical knowledge hurts salespeople. I disagree with both thoughts. I believe the more you understand your product or service and are able to EDUCATE your customer, the more successful you will become.

Bone up on all the details you can in regard to features, maintenance, operations, equipment, and history. When you think you know it all forwards and backwards, get to know how each of these areas impacts on your prospect. **What are the *benefits?***

Consumers confronted with a sales opportunity ask themselves four questions.

- What is it?
- How will it make my life easier or better?
- Can you prove it?
- What does it cost? Or more importantly, what is the Value?

Just like the telemarketers, be ready for questions your clients will throw out at you beforehand. Write down every possible objection you have ever heard and write up a strong benefit response.

This is true for consumers and business customers too.   If you don't have an answer prepared, get it. And if you can't get it on the spot, let your prospect know that you will get back to them as soon as possible...and then do it! But then document that information so you will have it on hand for the next time.

Nothing is worse than making a promise and failing to deliver. If you say you'll provide information within a certain time frame, stick to it. If you agree to call at a certain time, don't be late.

Every time you deliver on a promise, no matter how small,
it reflects positively on your offer

You want your clients to know that you are a guru of the product or service you are offering. The good news is that over time, patterns will begin to emerge as to the typical questions being asked. This gives you an even better opportunity to prepare your information-packed response and firm up your position as an expert.

The more knowledgeable you are, <u>the more comfortable they will feel</u> doing business with you. A comfortable prospect is a trusting prospect and a trusting prospect is just a step away from making a positive decision.

If you've done your homework and know your product/service inside and out, answering a prospect's questions (and making a sale) will be a cakewalk. If you *haven't* taken time to get to know your product, it's likely your prospect won't give you the time to make a sale.

Believe In Yourself and Your Product
Do you believe in what you sell? Do you know in your heart that what you are offering is good for the client or better for them than anything else? If you don't, your client will rightly identify your offer as insincere or not their best option and not do business with you.

Step Into Action
I hope you now understand the importance of product knowledge and how you can use what you know to polish your professional image and to give your offer more substance. And while knowledge is power, knowledge without action won't bring you success.

It's easy to get excited about how something works, but the real thrill comes from **practical application.** In this and every Tactical Area, you must **consistently put knowledge into action** in order to see results.

Action Step #1 – KNOW YOUR PRODUCT/BE THE EXPERT

Have you been stumped by a prospective client who has posed a question and you've had to hem and haw and finally say, "Can I get back to you on that?" How did you *feel* when that happened? More importantly did your client lose confidence in you at that point?

This is dangerous territory for someone trying to make a sale. You need to be the expert, especially right now. You may not get them back on the phone or in front of them again. Your ability translates itself to your prospect in a million different ways. So it's important that you see yourself as someone who's a <u>product 'expert'</u> not 'just' a salesperson.

Write a strong sales script and practice it dozens of times. Do the same thing with every potential question and possible rebuttal. Make sure you use smooth, simple and benefit focused language. Use testimonials if at all possible. Refer to past clients who had the same concerns and explain the positive outcome.

The other part of knowing your product and being the Product Expert is communicating that expertise to the client so god-forbid, if they are talking to another sales person, they will recognize that you are the expert and they will want to work with you.

Become the educator. When you are communicating with your clients or prospects keep them informed on new changes in the industry and about your services. Explain to them how these changes or upgrades will help their business and their bottom line.

ESTABLISH A USP (UNIQUE SELLING PROPOSITION)
Sit down and brainstorm with your staff and colleagues about
elements that should be included in your USP. Don't judge
the ideas, just write them down. Stimulate discussion with
questions like:

- What do we do the best?
- What do we do better than our competition?
- What awards have we won?
- What have our customers said about us?
- What praise do we often get from our customers?
- What endorsements for celebrities or well know
  organizations do we have? What endorsements could
  we get?
- What does our product or service do, better than
  anyone else's?
- How is our business model different from our
  competition?
- What market category or niche is not being served by
  our industry?

Learn everything possible about your company and the
product or service you are selling. I know it seems like a very
basic suggestion, but how much do you *really* know about
what you are selling? In a competitive market (and that goes
for any market you are in), you must constantly strive to
maintain your position as an expert if you want to be
successful.

Action Step #2 – TALK TO THE EXPERTS
Two heads are better than one, and if one of those heads is a
department head or supervisor or manager, it's better still. A
smart way to learn more about your product and your
company is to **periodically take an expert from another
department to lunch**.

Do you have an engineering department or even marketing support staff? These are the <u>people who are spending time looking towards the future</u> and deciding what you will be selling. They should know where the market is going to and you want to **access that information as early on as possible.**

This will put you on the leading edge of a new wave you might be able to ride to success.

Action Step #3 – TAKE ADVANTAGE OF LEARNING OPPORTUNITIES

Learning everything you can, will **increase your confidence** tremendously and that confidence will clearly set you apart. Plus by being able to answer all questions immediately you **eliminate a reason for your prospect to delay** making a decision.

If your company mounts a **training session,** prints **informational pamphlets**, or offers a weekend **seminar on a new business function**, be the first in line to sign up. You'll also want to consider **re-attending a training session** you've taken in the past just to make sure that nothing new has been added and that you haven't forgotten something important.

Introduction To Action Plans and Progress Reports

Every journey begins with a first step...and you now know the 3 easy steps to take to achieve success in this **Tactical Arena #1 – Superior Product Knowledge**

But...

Knowing what to do and actually *doing* something are two different things. So at the end of each Tactical Arena, I'm going to challenge you to lay out an Action Plan and keep track of your progress.

To create your action plan, **make a commitment to yourself** that you will do something tangible in the next hour, day, week, etc. to achieve your goals. Once you've shaken hands with yourself on that and **agreed to a consistent, ongoing plan of action,** then it's time to write down the three steps above on the page below or on a separate sheet of paper (or papers.)

Under each of the 3 steps, put down 5 bullet marks. Every time you **accomplish something** that moves you further on your journey, be sure to write it down alongside one of those bullets.

Put down the date that you took action and *the date that your action yielded results.* That way you'll see exactly how far you've moved along with each step.

What do you do when you run out of bullet points? Pat yourself on the back and **start all over again.** Remember, you're committed to a consistent, ongoing plan of action. If you successfully achieve your first goal, create a new one with a new set of steps and a progress report to match.

Please don't treat this as a throw-away step. It's anything but. Keeping a log of your actions makes it **impossible to lie to yourself**. You'll be able to see in black and white where you've honored your **commitment to success** and where you need to try harder.

Workspace for 3 Action Steps to Superior Product Knowledge

ACTION # 1

ACTION # 2

ACTION # 3

Tactical Arena #2 —Superior Customer Knowledge

As you are no doubt aware, there is often a tremendous gap about what we *think* is true and reality. Nowhere is this more often true than in the world of sales and marketing. Businesses die by the thousands, killed by either ignorant or arrogant owners who are convinced that they know 'what works.' Rather than being guided by facts, they're content to follow their instincts...right into oblivion.

The wiser course is to conduct **customer research**. The goal of your research is to help you craft your sales message in a style and tone that speaks directly and intimately to your target audience.

You don't have to hire a high-priced firm to conduct your customer research. There are lots of free and inexpensive ways to get information on your target audience and what makes them tick.

The first source for market knowledge is so obvious that many business people overlook it entirely: existing advertising. Companies of every shape and size advertise in magazines, online with pay-per-click ads, on billboards, in direct mail packages, etc.

Review the ads that are currently speaking to your target audience to get a sense of the tone you should use, as well as the words and phrases that push this market segments 'hot buttons.' How do you know what is working? That's usually easy to figure out, because it's the ads that have been running the most and the longest. **At this point try to focus on the message that is reaching the customers, not on the competition itself.** We will focus on the competition next chapter.

These also do not need to be ads for the same products you are selling. For example, if you are selling swimming pools, you could look at non-pool ads for high end home owners in other verticals such as Financial Planning, Insurance, or even Landscape services. What are the market leaders in these other verticals communicating to your potential customers?

While <u>market knowledge will not guarantee success</u>, questions about product position, pricing, product name, distribution, promotion, retail location and a host of other questions are often answered, at least in part, through market knowledge studies.

Success in sales is as much a result of **good information management** as it is a result of a good sales pitch. In fact, competitive intelligence will get you further than just a good sales pitch.

Actually, success in sales and everything else is a result of action. So let's get on to the three action steps you can take in this Tactical Arena...

3 Action Steps to Get Market-Focused NOW

Step #1 – GET TO KNOW WHY YOUR CUSTOMERS NEED YOU

When you sell your product or service how much do you know about how and why your product is needed within the company or consumer you are selling to? Do you really understand what the advantages and benefits are to the users? The most successful salespeople understand this better than the people they are selling to.

Learn everything you can about **how your products are used** within the users you are selling to and the markets they are in. Do your products make them money or are they a cost of doing business or are you a luxury they will increase their self-esteem?

Learn who your customers are, why they purchase from you and **what keeps them buying from you rather than your competitors**. This doesn't mean you need to know EACH customer individually rather you want to know **what types of people** buy from you.

In short, you want to **develop customer profiles**. To do that, you'll need to identify the information you really need and create your surveys. Identify some **core questions** and as you do your customer research write down and track your results.

Here are a few basic examples.

Core questions (demographics) for **business prospects** include:

- What industry are they in?

- What size is their company?
- What is their job title or function?
- What challenges does their industry currently face?

Core questions (demographics) for **consumer prospects** include:

- Where do they live? (City, state or country)
- What are their gender, age-range, education level and household income?
- What are their hobbies and interests?
- What does my product do to make their life better, easier or more enjoyable?

Step #2 – GET TO KNOW YOUR VERTICAL MARKETS

Typically, 'markets' are defined by specific industries: healthcare, pet products, automotive, etc. But vertical markets are those defined by the **type of customer** rather than by the type of product.

For example the traditional 'business software market' can be broken down into several areas based on the software user: accounting software, CRM software, productivity software, etc. Or on the consumer side your vertical market might be home owners, upper income, motorcycle enthusiasts.

Specializing in vertical markets can be an important way of **differentiating products and services** and crafting sales messages that speak to the unique needs of consumers within each vertical 'stripe.' Since the needs of customers may vary between vertical markets, it may be possible to **design or modify products to better address those needs.**

Jack Of All Trades, Master of None

Learn everything you can about the challenges your customers are facing. Sign up for all the **trade publications** your prospects might read. **Register for email alerts** that would be of interest to them. **Attend a conference or local show** within the industries in your vertical market.

Be careful that you don't spread yourself too thin. It's wise to limit your focus to **one or two vertical markets** and then become an expert on them. It's more useful to learn all you can about the challenges your customers are facing in one or two markets than to try and wrap your head around all the customers in all the markets. If you are selling to consumers face to face focus on specific geo areas to have better coverage. Of course if you are using the phone to prospect and sell, geographic areas have less importance.

After you master one or two vertical markets and are selling effectively to the consumers in those areas, you can move up to the next level and the next and the next.

Step #3 – LET YOUR VERTICAL MARKETS GET TO KNOW YOU

Your customers want information and credible advice. What they DON'T want is a sales pitch. The best way to overcome the fears that keeps consumers from buying is to educate them. When you focus your marketing efforts on educating, the customer it's called **Education-Based Marketing (EBM).**

EBM is a way to sell without selling.

How much education is required? Good question! It varies from product to product. The amount of education you need to give to a prospect is based on the <u>value</u> of your products or services and the <u>customer's awareness</u> of your products or services.

But make no mistake about it the more informed a consumer feels, the more likely he/she is to buy *now.* And that's exactly what you need to make your business (and your profits) grow.

Once you get to know your vertical markets, **let your vertical markets know you.** Showcase your talents and knowledge in places where your target prospects 'gather.' Try writing articles on your area of expertise.

Not a writer? Then share articles from **trade publications or whitepapers** with your email list. This will position you as generous resource and the kind of professional your prospects will want to talk to **when they're ready to do business.**

Workspace for 3 Action Steps to Superior Market Focus

Action step 1

Action step 2

Action step 3

Tactical Arena #3 – Superior Understanding of Your Competition

In thinking about selling a product or service, ask yourself one question:

Who is my competition?

Chances are you have a lot more competitors than you think. In addition to real competitors, evaluate the marketing tools and materials of any businesses your prospects perceive as offering a similar set of products or services.

For example, a custom cabinetmaker may believe he competes exclusively with other companies that build kitchen cabinets to order. But if his prospects think of the customized cabinetry offered by major home centers as competitive products, the cabinetmaker must evaluate the way the major chains market cabinetry in his local area

The old adage "keep your friends close, and your enemies closer" is applicable not only to personal relationships but business relationships as well. While I'm not suggesting that you befriend your competitors, it is important that you are aware of your competitors' business ventures and methods.

Covert Intelligence

There are several ways to conduct **competitive intelligence operations.** While it is fanciful to imagine yourself as a secret agent or spy, none of these techniques are difficult, hidden or secretive.

A wide range of research tools and services are available to all businesses. They range from expensive to moderately-priced to cost-free. The reason there are so many 'tools of the trade' for business research is a reflection of the immeasurable value of the information that you gain.

Knowing what the competition does right (and wrong), what they charge for their products or services, and where they seem to be headed can **give your business a significant boost.**

The good news is that it isn't difficult or expensive to discover this. As in many areas for 21st Century businesses, technology has leveled the playing field. A few simple, FREE searches on the Internet can provide you with priceless information that you can use to outmaneuver the competition.

Specifically look at the Top 3 most successful companies in your industry and study their advertising. What are they selling and who are they selling to? What market position did they take, high end/higher priced or value? Then compare that to your own companies advertising and marketing. What key points are you each focusing on? The same points or different aspects of your product's benefits? Can your product or service fill in a missing piece or need in the market?

Market place information
A 2nd great source for information comes from news sources and the equity markets. Certainly not every company is big enough to be covered in the news and not every company is publicly held, but quite a few are. If you are competing with a publicly held company get every bit of information you can from their prospectus or websites. Look for forward looking information telling you where they plan to go regarding new markets and investments. You may even want to buy a couple shares of stock to stay informed.

Cartoon strip character Pogo once said, "I have met the enemy and he is us" applies here. Your competition is a business just like you. And in order to effectively do battle in the marketplace, the more you know about your competition's arsenal the better prepared you'll be to win the fight for profits.

Enough theory! Let's move on to the action. That's where the profits are.

WORK SPACE FOR 3 ACTION STEPS TO SUPERIOR MARKET FOCUS.

3 Action Steps to Understand Your Competition NOW

Step #1 – HUNT AND GATHER
The first step in a competitive analysis is to gather your competitors' marketing tools and materials. Examine their web pages, print and broadcast advertising, and articles in which they've been featured. Request their brochures, sell sheets and any collateral materials.

Depending on your industry, you may also be able to do some **mystery shopping**, which will allow you to experience what it's like to shop and buy from companies that sell similar products or services.

Attempt to know more about your competition than they know about themselves. Learn **their strengths and their weaknesses** so you can play off of them. Then determine your best niche. For example if they are larger than you, can they still provide the same response time or the attention to detail that you can? Of if they are smaller than you do they have the experience or the depth of resources?

Whatever the difference it can be turned around to your benefit if you think it through.

Seek out potential competitors online, in the phone book, and in newspaper/magazine ads. Select 3-5 or 5-10 of the **businesses that are doing well** and try to determine the features or services that they stress in their messages.

Once you've gathered the materials, the next step is to analyze what's being communicated and how. Identify the key promises made by your broad field of competitors. And don't be surprised if you see a lot of "me too" marketing. There's so much out there that's mediocre or worse, you may find the majority of your competitors have similar messaging, with only a few front-runners showing strong points of differentiation.

After assessing the most effective messaging, look at the actual tools and materials themselves. What formats seem to work best overall? At this point, your competitive analysis will reveal whether your company is lacking any standard tools that prospects expect everyone in your industry to offer.

Now comes the **tricky part**: look for the gap in their products or services that you can bridge. What area of the market is *not* being serviced where you can make your mark? And most importantly, is there an opportunity to charge more (and make bigger profits) in a niche that's been ignored?

Step #2 – STAY UP TO DATE.
Competitive information is only valuable if it's current. Whenever possible, sign up for alerts from online news agencies about your competition. Dun & Bradstreet or Hoosiers can send you **updates on changes (financial or otherwise)** about your competition.

Identify where you fit in the competitive landscape to determine your best niche. Use their size to your advantage. If you are in smaller or local markets do regular Google searches to see if anything pops up.

And always **read your trade publications** and consult **local business resources** to see what's going on in your industry. Never assume you will hear everything you need to know. One change at a competitor can provide you with opportunities or it might mean you will need to adjust your sales presentation and   to keep selling.

Step #3 – BUY STOCK

If it is appropriate, you should consider buying one share of stock of your competition so you can receive updates and alerts on them. Some companies issue an annual **prospectus** and **quarterly reports**. It's incredible how much information is available if you look for it.

Workspace for 3 Action Steps to Superior Understanding of the Competition

Tactical Arena #4 – Defined Goal-Setting

Every person who sells has a quota or a sales goal. Some are set by our companies and some we set ourselves. But how many of us have actually created a **detailed plan** that will help us realize our goals? The more defined you can be the easier it will be to measure where you are on the path to success.

This is one of the biggest secrets to successful telemarketing; constant measurement of every single number on an hourly and daily basis.

Many salespeople create goals, but very few have integrated specific goal-setting criteria into their **goal planning, goal setting and goal achievement process**. If you don't already know it, this is your chance to learn the **S.M.A.R.T.** criteria for goal-setting success

- **S** - **Specific goals you can define**
- **M** - **Measurable goals you can quantify**
- **A** - **Attainable goals you can reach**
- **R** - **Realistically high goals that will challenge you.**
- **T** - **Target Date/Time Driven goals you can meet**

The S.M.A.R.T. criteria for goal setting success has a corollary known as **W.H.Y.**

- **W – Write Down Your Goals:** Write your goals down, update them constantly based on your real results, then make them public and display them close by. Studies show that people who share their goals with others are **70% more likely to achieve them**.

Share your goals with those people you respect the most, and you'll work harder to ensure that you don't disappoint them.

- **H – Habituate Your Goal Planning:** Additionally, goal planning, setting and achievement is a process that should become a Habit of behavior. Weekly written grocery lists or the daily "to do" lists are habits that improve performance. Planning, setting and executing sales goals should become a habit that is consistently demonstrated and reviewed on a weekly, monthly and yearly basis.

- **Y – Your Goals Are What Count:** Achieving someone else's goals isn't satisfying; achieving *your* goals is what counts. So when the business sales goals can be translated into your specific goals, then you have greater ownership of the goals. That means don't just say I want $1 Million in sales. Say I will hit $1 Million in sales because it will provide me (fill in the blank).

Goal-setting catapults you into action. With your destination determined, it's time to consider all the possible paths that can be taken to help you get there. Evaluate these paths and **calculate all possible consequences** that may unfold and which may throw obstacles onto your route. Work backwards to think about what is needed, to meet your goals.

Now "I want to go to the moon", is a goal that at first glance looks literally like a pie in the sky idea. But if you take it backwards step by step and document what is needed, like this, maybe it's not.

- Go to the moon.
- Work at NASA
- Be a pilot in the Air force.

- Earn an advanced science degree in College.
- Score highest in Math & Science in High School.
- Challenge myself with the hardest Math & Science classes
- Ask my teachers for extra help so I can earn A's.
- Do research to find out what is necessary to be a Pilot & Scientist.

But followed by step by step processes that details what needs to happen to get to the moon, now you are turning unbelievably tough goals from a possibility into a likely outcome.

SHARE YOUR GOALS

When you think you've got a winning goal strategy...step back from it for a minute. <u>Review your plan</u> and if possible have a <u>close friend or associate have a look at it also</u>, and offer you a second set of eyes.

Warning!
If you do go for the **second opinion** and have set a high goal for yourself, many people will have a knee-jerk negative reaction. "You'll never be able to do that!" Be prepared for criticism when trying to break away from the norm of regular day to day life. Listen to what people have to say, determine if you are missing any important details and then make your own decision about any changes or adjustments.

It's been said that, "Hard work is its own reward." That may be true. But hard work is far more satisfying when you know what you're working for. The difference between top sales performers and the rest of the field is clear. Top performers have **goals and a plan to achieve them**, and they **act on that plan each and every day.**

This year, commit yourself to being a top performer. Start by establishing your annual goals. Then design a working plan that you can review and refine each day, each week, and each month. With this approach, you're in a prime position to

Move towards your goals consistently, monitor your results,
and fine-tune your efforts to maximum success.

The goal of this book is to get you to act....to begin the processes that will help you double your sales NOW as the title suggests. So let's move on to the 3 Action Steps that will help you in this Tactical Area...

3 Action Steps to Superior Goal Setting

Step #1 - SET LONG-TERM GOALS
How many new sales will you generate this year? What percentage of your current accounts will you retain and resell and how many will need to be replaced? Calculate the revenue dollars per account per year you will generate and then the dollars you will earn off of each account.

This information is based on the past. And while goal-setting is about the future, good goal-setting never loses sight of the past. In order to set realistic goals for *this* year, you must look long and hard at what you've achieved previously and be willing to make big changes to improve your outcome.

REMEMBER WHAT Einstein said. Insanity is doing the same thing over and over and expecting a different outcome. You have to make daily changes if you want to change the outcome.

Define your yearly objective and make this definition quantifiable. Saying, "I want to sell more" sounds good, but means nothing. However if you get specific -- "I want to close $1,000,000 in new business and $1,000,000 in existing client repeat business this year" – you have a precise goal you can work to achieve.

All Work and No Play...
You may be a sales 'machine,' but you're also a human being. And while it's important to stay focused on your professional goals, you don't want to sacrifice your life on the altar of business. It's important that you enjoy the money you earn.

So include personal goals in your annual plan. Even when you have big sales goals you need to take a day or two every week to rest, relax and rejuvenate. You also have to plan Holiday & Vacation time. Then enjoy your time off. You earned it!

Step #2 - SET INTERIM GOALS

Are you on track to meet your yearly revenue goals? When you fall behind – or advance – it's important to make adjustments both in your goals and your processes. If the first quarter started off slow, what will it take to still get you at the end of the year and reach your projected income figures?

You will only achieve your annual goals if you meet your interim goals – daily, weekly, and monthly. When you create interim goals, you create opportunities to stop and look at the progress you've made. You can analyze whether your projections were on-target or whether you need to do something differently in order to get where you want to be.

Interim goal-setting help you know when you need to adjust. If you're clear about your expectations and continue to monitor your results each day, week, and month, there won't be any unpleasant surprises or "How did this happen?" questions at year's end.

For people used to making five-year and ten-year plans, daily goal setting may seem a little extreme. But take my work for it...it's not.

A month can seem so long, but in most cases it's only 22 working days. Those days have a funny way of zooming past you and before you know it, you've missed your sales target.

That's why you need to **work backwards from your yearly goals** and determine your working plan for each day.

YOU NEED TO KNOW YOUR METRICS. I DON'T KNOW THEM. YOU NEED TO FIGURE THEM OUT.

What I mean by that is how many calls does it take to get an appointment? Then how many appointments does it take to get a Sale?

Let's say you want to generate 100 new accounts a year and you know that it takes 500 in- person presentations to do that. In turn, you'll need to make 2500 initial telephone contacts to make that happen. To achieve this yearly goal, you need to talk to 10 people a day...not taking account for sick days, vacation days and days you just don't feel like cold calling.

Again you need to figure this out because the number changes with every industry. And if you don't know what it takes you can say you want to generate a certain $ amount in sales, but it's not going to happen.

Think of the long-term impact if you start to fall behind. Imagine being behind for the week and having to do 50 calls...or being behind for the month and needing to do 200 calls.

Some people are so overwhelmed at the thought of what they need to accomplish in a year that they get stuck and don't do anything. It's unfortunate and unnecessary. When you break down big tasks into more manageable hunks, the work gets done. When you set and meet daily goals, your weekly, monthly, and yearly goals will naturally take care of themselves.

When you have your daily goals in place, you can **use your time to best advantage.** You can write proposals when you feel fresh, contact clients when they're at their desks, schedule business luncheons and breakfasts, etc.

Interim goal setting helps you accomplish more so you can sell more...

...and live more, too.

When you have a big picture view of your goals and the ability to 'thrust and parry' (adjust) your daily goals, you can make time for yourself when you need to. With your flexible approach to interim goal setting, you can 'miss a day' and still be on track for the week, the month, and the year.

It's a lot easier to take a day off if you are ahead, then to play catch up.

Step #3 – KEEP DETAILED PROGRESS REPORTS
Successful sales people record their progress toward each goal every day, and then list the five most important things they need to do the next day to move that goal even further ahead. This short list is 100% focused on achieving goals, because the most effective salespeople understand that

Daily discipline is the key to success.

(But you already know that don't you. You've begun to map out your own progress reports in the **Workspace for Action Steps** at the end of each chapter.)

Give Yourself a Pat on the Back
Tasks that are **rewarded** are tasks that get done. Work to create a **rewards system** that keep you motivated and on track for meeting daily, weekly, and monthly goals. Pick

something that is truly meaningful to you and only reward yourself when you meet your goal.

I had one friend who was a real coffee fiend. She was very committed to success...and very committed to her daily Starbucks fix...but hating making cold calls for her real estate business. This woman made a deal with herself: **no coffee before calls**. Starbucks was off-limits until she completed her daily complement of 10 sales calls.

Guess what gets done first thing each morning? Remember the early bird gets the worm. I hate old clichés, but they are based on consistent truth.

Workspace for 3 Action Steps to Superior Goal-Setting

Tactical Arena #5 – Superior Sales Preparation and Planning

This guide was designed to put you on the cutting edge of sales effectiveness in the 21st Century, but it borrows heavily on ideas and theories that have been working for hundreds of years. One of those theories is 'If you fail to prepare, then you should prepare to fail' and it rings as true today as when it was first said (probably when dinosaurs walked the earth!)

Many sales professionals expect to surpass sales quotas become top producers and achieve success without adequate preparation. This lack of preparation results in frustration and discouragement.

You can't prepare until you know what you want to accomplish. You need a starting point and an endpoint, and all the steps in between. Don't trust the critical details to your memory...**create a written plan**. A written plan is a powerful tool when it comes to achieving goals.

The secret to written plans is that they are *not written in stone.* Your plans, especially the short range ones, will change constantly in response to your real life experiences. For example, it's fine to plan to give a 10-minute telephone sales pitch to prospective clients, but if experience teaches you that people only stay on the line for 5...you need to change you plans to achieve your goals.

When it comes to your goals...think BIG. As a sales professional, you should challenge yourself with **above-average goals** that are also **realistic.**

Know What The Finish Line Looks Like

Long term where do you want to be? How successful do you want to be? Put a number to it. Do you want to earn $50,000 per year or $500,000? Or maybe it's $5,000,000. Do you want to make one sale a week or a hundred? Whatever it is, decide and then **develop a plan for effective selling** and **prepare to sell**.

Let me ask you something. Are you **passionate about selling your product/service?**

If you're not enthusiastic about sharing the 'good news' of your product/service with the world, then you will find the time and effort required to prepare for selling unsatisfying . If you're not passionate about the sales process and are simply going through the motions mechanically, it will feel like drudgery...like 'work' in the worst sense of the word.

Financial need provides <u>motivation but not passion</u>. 'Paying the rent' is a reason to make money, but it's not a reason to be passionate about the product or service you're selling.

Passion provides motivation. That makes it easier to sell and to prepare to sell. And to be perfectly honest:

> **If you are not passionate about selling your product, your prospect will not be passionate about buying it.**

When you're *truly* excited about what you're selling, it's easy to turn the 'work' of planning into a labor of love. When you've got your plan in hand, it's time to **prepare.**

Pitch Perfect
Planning and preparation go hand in hand. You decide what you want to achieve and then you review, review, and review again all the steps that you'll need to take, practicing over and over until you're 'pitch perfect.'

Ready, Willing, and "Able To"

I've quoted other people's adages in this guide, and now here's one of my own: "When you prepare to sell with passion, you should also prepare for the wave of success that will follow." **The worst thing that can happen is for you to be unable to meet your demand.**

All your hard work will go down the drain and it is unlikely that you will ever be able to win back the customers you disappointed.

What you will do to 'practice' for selling will take on a different meaning in different sales environments. If you are giving a sales presentation that will have you standing in front of a group of a hundred people narrating a Powerpoint slide show, you would practice using a microphone, practice manipulating the slides, practice fielding questions from the audience, and most of all practicing until you can **present yourself flawlessly**.

If you're giving a one-to-one sales pitch, practice could include getting your handshake just right (so that it's firm, without being overpowering). You'll also go over the points you want to make so that you may speak naturally and not sound like you're reading.

Whatever the milieu, practice and preparation make perfect...a perfect sales pitch where you seal the deal effortlessly and consistently. 'Adequate preparation' is how C-students coast through school and average salespeople stay trapped in mediocrity. On the flip side,

Superior preparation yields superior results.

This chapter has prepared you to take action . To do that, here are three of the steps you can take right away to becoming a superior person...or at least a superior SALESperson:

3 Action Steps to Prep and Plan for Sales NOW

Step #1 – BE A CLOCK WATCHER

When you don't <u>prioritize your selling time,</u> you're 100% more likely to miss golden opportunities. For example, if you are in business-to-business sales, the best time to reach your prospects is probably between 10AM and 3PM. (If you were trying to reach bartenders, the clock would shift.)

This window of opportunity is well-known and quite established as the right time for prospecting and selling. Yet it is surprisingly common to find salespeople working on spreadsheets, researching market info, reviewing sales figures, etc. during this golden time. Why? Because it's easy!

Prospecting is hard and (here's another one of those sayings) "We're only human." As humans, we like to do what's easy. So many people get wrapped up doing busy work (like filing) because it gives them a sense of accomplishment without too much effort.

A sense of accomplishment is fine. A pocket full of signed sales orders is better. Don't take the easy way out.

Know the prime time for selling in *your* niche and punch the clock daily!

Stick to a schedule that only allows **person-to-person selling activities during prime selling time.** If you work in an office, get your co-workers to adopt the same philosophy. Make sure everybody is free and encouraged to <u>remind each other</u> when someone falls off the wagon.

Set daily prospecting and sales goals and **never allow non-selling activities to get in the way of making sales.**

Step #2 – GET SCRIPTED

Before you walk in the door, pick up the phone or make any type of sales presentation, you must plan, prepare, and practice your message. **Write a sales script.** Think about your message from start to finish and write down <u>exactly what you will say</u> to present the specific benefits that will connect with your prospect.

This is a critical learning step for people who are new to sales. It is also an invaluable **self-diagnostic** for people who may have been selling a long time. It's easy to lose your edge when you do something over and over. So even if you've made a thousand sales presentations, <u>do this 'exercise' at least once a year.</u>

I have seen and heard some very experienced salespeople who think they are getting their message across effectively, but are actually coming across as stale and boring. *Don't let this happen to you!* Challenge yourself to <u>maximize your presentation and message</u> to be as effective as possible. All it takes is a few, well-spent hours crafting

**A finely tuned message that focuses on the biggest benefit you offer
and educates customers as to why they must choose your product**

In addition to creating a sales- and action-oriented message, you should also create **standardized responses that overcome objections effectively**. What are the most common rebuttals or reasons that prospects might give when they refuse your offer? Write them down and then script a response.

Las Vegas comedians may be good with quick comebacks, but that's because they practice! They know it's tough coming back with the perfect response when you are in the middle of a presentation and the adrenaline is pumping.

Business is no laughing matter, but everyone involved in sales can learn from the funny people. When you plan and practice responses ahead of time, you sound more confident and the ease you exhibit is what helps convince customers that you are an expert.

Step #3 – PRACTICE WHAT YOU'LL PREACH
For all of us who have been selling for years, this is another point that you may believe you can pass over. You would be surprised at how wrong you are. It's important to **audiotape, videotape, and 'role play' your presentation regularly** to maximize your effectiveness.

A sales presentation is a performance. And like other 'performers' – from actors to lawyers to teachers – you need to hone your craft until you've perfected it. Sir Laurence Olivier practiced his lines repeatedly. You should to. And don't forget...

Ask for feedback on your presentation.

Certainly we all have our own way of presenting and connecting with our customers. But almost every one can use feedback. Invite your sales manager, your partner or a trusted co-worker to listen to your sales calls, watch your video presentation or to go with you on a sales call.

This is no time to get sensitive! When you ask for feedback, listen to it, <u>don't be defensive</u> or you'll be wasting everyone's time. Be open to feedback, weigh it, consider it...and then **decide how valid it is.** It's up to *you* to determine whether you should act on what you've learned.

**Workspace for 3 Action Steps to Superior Sales
Planning and Preparation**

Tactical Arena #6 – Superior Daily Selling Activities

Salespeople, like anybody else, like to perform certain tasks more than others. Some may love data entry, others may love preparing quotes and still others may love researching prospect information on the Internet. All of these things may indeed be integral parts of the sales process; however, unless you're in a situation that can't wait, all of these tasks should be performed during non-prime time hours.

One of the mantras you should add to your list is **I will prioritize selling as a daily activity.**

Speaking philosophically, activity creates movement in the Universe. Even the smallest butterfly moves air. Speaking practically, even the smallest sales effort creates movement in the profit-making universe.

You need to do something every single day to **keep the sales cycle moving along.** Cold calls, email, prospect letters, asking for referrals, etc. Even on bad days, you can always do something to keep your name out there.

One-a-Day
Surprisingly, just **one sale a day**, depending on the purchase price, can lead to a lot of money down the road. The question is,

How can you go about getting one sale per day?

It doesn't seem like something that should be so hard. The truth is, it's not hard. As a matter of fact, once you've figured out how to make the first sale, the rest of them should come very easily.

If you're scratching your head and saying, "I'm in sales. Sales is always a part of my daily activity," you're missing the point. The root of the word 'activity' is act...and being a salesperson isn't the same as selling every day.

Showing up for work each day, making calls, setting up appointments and meeting clients is part of the picture, but only part...the hopeful part. When your daily activity is just showing up, going through the motions of sales, and crossing your fingers that something good will happen -- like some sales – you're on a fast track to failure.

Bill Clinton may have come from a place called "Hope," but successful salespeople come from a different place...a place of action in addition to hope. I think of it as a place called "Make It Happen."

What Will I Do Today?
So what should you include in your daily sales plan? If you want to be a top producer you'll need to do what top producers do:

- **Work on yourself to improve your sales 'game' (technique)**
- **Know the daily goals or targets that you're working to achieve**
- **Develop self-motivation and self-leadership skills**

You'll need to do all that on top of the specific sales activities. It's not difficult, but it does require work and dedication. That's why there are so few at the top. But if you have the discipline, the drive, and the desire...you can be one of the few, too.

The key is to be focused...focused on today.

When you're only focused on today and you make today a success, the payoff you receive goes beyond dollars and cents. Daily success makes you feel really good about yourself and about the day itself. And as one success links to another like the beads of a necklace, you suddenly realize that you're created a **string of success** with no end in sight.

That's very motivating...**motivation is good.**

Action is also good. So do not pass Go, do not collect $200. Just go directly to the next page and the 3 Action Steps that will support your success in this Tactical Area.

3 Action Steps to Improve Daily Selling Activities NOW

Step #1 – CREATE YOUR 'TO DO' LIST DAILY...AT NIGHT

The morning tends to hold the most productive work hours of the day. Your mind is refreshed after a good night's sleep (hopefully) and all systems are fueled up with a good breakfast (hopefully). You're ready to blast off.

It would be a shame to waste all that energy and enthusiasm on creating your To Do list for the day. Instead, organize your thoughts and create your game plan at the *end* of the day.

Before you shut down operations each evening, spend a few minutes getting organized for the following day. Tidy up your desk, your emailbox, your briefcase, etc. so that everything is ready to go when you first arrive.

Take stock of what you've achieved and **what your priorities will be throughout the day.** As you create your work plan, I recommend that you put your thorniest challenge at the top of the list so you can give it your attention first thing. It could be visiting the office of a dissatisfied customer, analyzing the results of a recent sales initiative, ordoing your quarterly business taxes.

Whatever it is, I guarantee you that if you **get it out of the way,** the rest of your day will seem easy.

Deciding what *not* to do is almost as important as deciding what *to* do each day. It's important that you have your game plan in place so that you aren't sidetracked before you even begin. A 'To Do' list and a 'Not To Do' list help you hit the ground running as soon as your workday begins.

Don't To It...Ever

In addition to a daily To Do list, many successful people I know use **permanent 'Not To Do' lists.** Business life is filled with wasted time and effort. Time-wasters are any activities that are not actively moving your sales goals forward. Checking scores, the stock market, and AOL's online news headlines may yield interesting information, but they are still time wasters. (Do you really need to know the latest about Britney Spears?)

Even reading the newspaper for some people is a time waster. Certainly you need to **keep abreast of current events,** but do you need to read the metro section and learn about all the depressing robberies or murders? Post a sign above your computer monitor to remind you "Prime time is selling time. Now get back to work!" Or my favorite,

"How much money did you make surfing the Internet today?"

I encourage you to think about your personal time wasters and vow to eliminate them from your day. Save time and skip things that steal time from you.

Step #2 – DIVERSIFY YOUR EFFORTS

You might have a day here or there when you will need to devote the entire day to a specific task. You may really need to finish a proposal or spend the day with a client. It happens. But most days should have a **variety of different activities** to keep you fresh.

Every one likes or dislikes some sales activities more or less than others. Unfortunately, many sales people have developed a very bad habit. They avoid what you don't like and do what they do like. Unfortunately, avoiding things like cold calls, follow-up, networking, etc. doesn't move you towards your goals.

Instead of avoiding tasks you dislike, break them down into small manageable chunks. That way even the most odious chore can be accomplished in a short amount of time. Think about it. Isn't it better to spend 30 minutes each day on cold calls rather than having to spend an entire week on the phone at the end of the month trying to drum up business and meet your sales goals?

Whether it's cold calling, writing, networking or sales calls make sure you are doing multiple things a day to **keep yourself engaged and moving towards your goals.**

Step #3 – COMPARTMENTALIZE YOUR PROSPECTS
The first would be your **dream prospects**. These are the biggest and possibly the toughest to reach and sell to. But they are also your best place to earn the big bucks. Maybe these companies are from the Fortune 500. Or if you are selling direct to consumers, maybe these are the Rockefellers who usually would only buy from personal references or someone they know.

Identify your 5 to 10 top prospects and build a knowledge base of information around them. Track everything you can about them like ownership, management, who the influencers are and their yearly and quarterly sales data. Be the first to know when they move into any new markets, have new opportunities or problems.

Know and understand more about their business than they do themselves.

These are the accounts that are going to generate the six-figure earnings for you...if not more. You may not be able to spend all of your time here because it usually takes longer to get a new account opened up. But try to devote **15 to 20% of your time** on these biggest opportunities.

Continually market, email, send postcards and make phone calls to these prospects. Stay in front of these biggest potential prospects. Even if they keep saying no, things change...things always change.

The second would be **medium difficulty and middle of the road** in terms of revenue potential. Certainly you can make a good living here, but you will need more accounts to make your yearly sales goals. Spend the bulk of your time here, maybe **60 or 65%.**

The third group would be **easy to sell but very low revenue potential.** Most new salespeople start with the third group. They are easier to reach, non- threatening and typically there are lot's of them out there.

Unfortunately because the revenue potential is low at a certain point you are just wasting your time with these people. It takes just as much time to service low-end clients and they can even be more demanding. Only spend **10% of your time** here.

Don't get me wrong! This is not a bad place to **cut your teeth and gain experience.** However, if you keep your focus on these smaller accounts you will have difficulty finding time to go after the large possibilities where you can substantially increase your income.

Some sales professionals never move on from this group. I would say to you if you've been in sales for more than 2 years drop this group entirely. I recommend that you focus on the dream prospects and middle-of-the-roaders, and you will **reach your sales revenue potential more easily.**

Workspace for 3 Action Steps to Superior Daily Selling Activities

Tactical Arena #7 – Superior Networking

Remember the old adage, it's now what you know but who you know? Networking is one of the best and sometimes easiest ways to double your sales. For some reason we all like to receive recommendations from friends or business associates when we look to buy.

There is a strong association between an entrepreneur as a person and his or her business. As a result, successful salespeople must out into the world and create and maintain a network of relationships, both business and personal, to

Put a human face on business

According to the Merriam Webster dictionary, a network is a "fabric or structure of cords or wires that cross at regular intervals and are knotted or secure at the crossings." If we rewrite that definition a bit for sales purposes, we could say that a network is a

A structure of people and contacts that cross at regular intervals
and are secure at the crossings.

The real power in networking comes from understanding a simple fact; **everyone you know and each person you meet knows on average 250 people**. Your goal in networking should not be to get the people you meet to become your customers - it should be to become a part of THEIR network, and for them to become a part of yours.

Direct vs. Indirect
There are two kinds of people you will meet when networking. Both are important. A **direct contact** is a decision-maker who can buy what you're selling. In my niche that would be a marketing manager or CEO of an organization. An **indirect**

contact could be anyone in an organization who has **a connection** to a direct contact.

Indirect contacts are great places to begin forging relationships. These people can include assistants, secretaries, supervisors and department chairs. But they can also be people who are linked to your direct contact in a more social way: members of the same organization, service providers, etc. And unlike decision-makers, indirect contacts are often **more accessible** and more willing to listen to your pitch.

In essence, you make an indirect contact part of your sales effort. The person becomes your partner...even if they don't realize it.

Know What You Want
Ask yourself what your goals are in participating in networking meetings so that you will <u>pick groups that will help you get what you are looking for</u>. Some activities are based more on learning and/or volunteering rather than on strictly making business connections.

You're Not There For the Snacks
It is very easy to attend a lot of events, have something to eat and drink, make small talk and walk away saying, "I've done my networking." Unfortunately 'socializing' is not the same as 'networking.' True networking requires **a professional approach to making contacts** and **a professional approach to following up with those contacts.**

Not every networking opportunity is a winner. I recommend that you visit as many groups as possible that spark your interest to determine if networking there will be effective, as well as possible. During your 'test run,' notice the tone and attitude of the group. Do the people sound supportive of one another? Is the activity well run and does the leadership appear competent?

Work It!

In many networking events, you will find yourself with time to mingle among the other attendees before the formal program begins. It may be beneficial for you to spend some time planning and preparing how you will "work the room" to get the most from your efforts.

- Spend some time planning your conversation generators.
- Start with small talk.
- Don't stay too long in one place.

Do's and Don'ts of Networking

- Do ask questions about the other person.

- Do ask if you can stay in touch.

- Do send a follow-up note, and touch on a few things you discussed.

- Do take active steps on a regular basis to strengthen your network by both staying in touch with people you've connected with, and by finding ways to connect with new people.

- Do use networking as one of many tools in your arsenal for effective prospecting.

- Do actively find ways to make connections between members of your network - remember making more and more connections is what it's all about.

- Do offer to do things for others in your network, even if there's no immediate promise of reward or reciprocation.

- Don't approach networking with the expectation of immediate gratification; your goal is to meet people and to understand as much about them as you can.

- Don't give people you meet for the first time a "sales pitch."

Networking Is A Two-Way Street

Don't get discouraged if you don't see things happen right away; true networks take time to build. Keep in mind that networking is about being genuine and authentic, **building trust and relationships**, and seeing

**How you can help others,
NOT how they can help you.**

Networking is different than selling. Unless you carry your product in your pocket along with a credit card swiper, you won't be making sales at networking events. Instead, you'll be laying the foundation for sales. When you network with giving as your goal (rather than selling), you will establish yourself as a **strong resource**, a **trusted friend,** and the professional people will turn to for suggestions, ideas, names of other people, etc.

When the time is right to buy what you're selling, the people you've helped in the past as part of your networking efforts will remember your kindness and **reward you with their business.**

There is no question that building a strong network can be incredibly helpful to your sales efforts. Nevertheless, many people in sales face the same difficulties in networking that they face in cold-calling. It sounds great, yet for some reason they just don't seem to be able to do it effectively.

All thought and no action makes Jack a dull boy and an non-success in the sales arena. (Jill, too). Fortunately, the following 3 Action Steps will help *you* be a do-er, not a dreamer.

3 Action Steps to Improve Networking NOW

Step #1 – BE A JOINER

The best networking results come from attending the appropriate **networking events for your particular industry**. This should include <u>trade shows, conferences, and associations</u> dedicated to your type of business. For example, if your target market is a Fortune 500 company, it does not make sense to join a group whose primary membership consists of individual business owners.

You can also participate in groups <u>where your potential clients meet</u>. A friend of mine helps people negotiate leases with their landlords. He joined the local franchise association because most franchisors lease their commercial space.

Step #2 – NETWORK WITH YOUR CUSTOMERS

Your satisfied customers provide an outstanding networking opportunity. They know your strengths and probably have contacts that are perfect for you. Referrals from existing customers are generally the easiest prospects to close. There is more trust and confidence on the part of the buyer because of the referral.

This fact alone can **cut the sales process in half**.

When you make a sale, hand over a business card with a friendly, "I've enjoyed doing business with you. I would appreciate a referral, if you know anyone that could use my services'. This open-ended appeal is soft and won't make your customer feel like he or she is on the spot.

People naturally like to do favors for people. Use psychology to your advantage and when you hand over your card, you can say, 'Could you do me a favor by referring my services to someone?" This is particularly effective with customers who feel you've gone the extra mile for them. They'll want to return the favor.

Step #3 – GET CARDED
Your business card is crucial to your sales success. Though tiny in size, they speak volumes about who you are, what you offer and how serious you are as a business. Never leave home without them.

Your networking checklist should be expanded to include business cards. Armed with your cards, you can turn any 'by chance' meeting into a networking opportunity. A morning run or a quick trip to the local store could be an opportunity to network.

Show That You Care
Whenever you give a business card, <u>ask for a business card.</u> When given a business card, don't just take it and place it in your pocket. Make the person feel important by looking at their card for a few seconds. You might see something that could be a topic of discussion.

Write comments on the card such as date, location and common points of interest. These comments will prove valuable when following up with that person. This also demonstrates a sincere interest in the other person. Then place it in your wallet. This lets them know they reside in a special place with you.

**Make people feel important in order to
make yourself important to them.**

Workspace for 3 Action Steps to Superior Networking

Tactical Arena #8 – Superior Relationship-Building

If real estate is all about location, location, location, then small business is all about relationships, relationships, relationships. Find them, nurture them, and watch your sales soar.

Whether you know it or not, you were born with **the natural ability to meet people and build relationships.** Even if you don't spend much time proactively building relationships, you should be able to point to numerous examples of relationship buildings such as with friends, co-workers, doctors, etc.

We are *all* born with the ability to connect; successful salespeople have simply learned to utilize this skill more than others. And that's good because relationship-building is how you can create **customers for life,** people who come to you again and again to satisfy their needs.

Before you spend your time and money going after new customers and clients, consider the following statistics:

- It costs six times more to sell something to a prospect than to sell that same thing to a customer.
- Repeat customers spend 33% more than new customers.
- Referrals are 107% greater from customers than non-customers.

Doing What Comes Naturally
Building relationships is easy and, in many ways, is a natural outgrowth of good business. All you need to do to bond with your customers is to **satisfy their needs and solve their**

problems with the right products and services. You want to reach out to them with the right messages at the right time.

Imagine every customer as a real person standing in front of you. What are his/her needs and how well are you addressing these needs? Let this image guide you in all aspects of your business and you'll discover hundreds of ways to form lasting customer relationships.

Remember, customers can easily detect indifference and insincerity in a business relationship. And since almost every niche is highly competitive, consumers know they can take their business elsewhere.

This makes building and maintaining loyalty a long-term challenge that you must strive for every day and with every transaction... no matter how big or small. But by placing the customer at the center of all your thinking you create an environment which fosters long term success

A business relationship is like a romantic relationship. You want to set yourself apart from the competition and show the customer that you are uniquely qualified to provide happiness, relief, satisfaction, entertainment, service, or whatever else is desirable.

Loyal customers are your best salespeople. So spend the time to build your network and do the follow-up. Today there are cost effective tools, like e-mail marketing, that make this easy. You can e-mail a simple newsletter, an offer or an update message of interest to your network (make sure it's of interest to them, not just to you). Then they'll remember you and what you do and deliver value back to you with referrals. They'll hear about opportunities you'll never hear about.

The only way they can say, "Wow, I met somebody who's really good at XYZ. You should give her a call," is if they remember you. Then your customers become your sales force.

According to the global management consulting firm Bain and Co.,

**A 5% increase in retention yields
profit increases of as much as 100%**

So your most profitable customers are repeat customers...the people with whom you've build a solid, enduring relationship. Are you doing all you can to encourage them to buy from you again?

Stay in touch, and give them something of value in exchange for their time, attention and business. You don't have to give until it hurts. In fact, providing information products, helpful insights and advice, or news customers can use to their advantage doesn't have to cost a lot, but the return on your investment can be significant.

Just remember...

If you don't keep in touch with your customers, your competitors will.

Once you've created you're A-List, it's time to bring your A-game. Create a series of relationship-building processes that will strengthen the ties that bind you together.

The following 3 Action Steps were designed with that goal in mind.

3 Action Steps to Improve Relationship-Building NOW

Step #1 – OFFER REWARDS

The strategy is simple: Give high-paying customers an incentive, and they'll come back and buy more. That way, you <u>boost sales, find new customers through referrals, and lower your costs</u> of marketing and customer acquisition.

There are dozens of '**premium' rewards** for customers. These include

- Frequent buyer clubs
- Buy-several-get-one-free offers
- Giveaways
- Time-sensitive promotions
- Discounts made available only to loyal customers.

Another way to deeper the connection is with **personalized rewards.** An ice cream emporium in my neighborhood offers a free scoop to patrons on their birthday. Remembering a customer with a card or gift on his/her 'special day' sends the message that you see your customer as an individual, not a wallet with eyes.

These relationship-builders are tried and true, but they're also costly.

Fortunately, <u>the best things in life are free</u>. Like the words "Thank you."

Want to establish a strong bond with a customer? Send a **personalized thank-you note**. After each visit or major purchase, send notes that thank the customer for his/her business. A simple expression of your gratitude is <u>very</u>

rewarding for the person who receives it. (And if you can include a discount coupon...all the better!

A personalized reward can also be news or sales dates for a **customer's preferred brand** or product will also make a favorable impression. The bottom line is that you can start to build long-term relationships by doing anything that lets your customer know,

> **"I appreciate your business and I'm going to express my gratitude in a tangible way."**

Step #2 – DO MORE THAN EXPECTED
One way to win a customer for life is to consistently exceed expectations.. Establish a baseline of good, and then make it policy to deliver something better...and beyond.

I think one of the best examples of this is illustrated in the movie "Miracle on 34th Street."

In that venerable film, a store Santa from Macy's tells a frantic mother than the holiday toy she wants is available at Gimbles, Macy's chief competitor. The mother is so delighted by the Santa's helpfulness that she promises to return to Macy's for all her future purches.

In this instance, Santa focused on Macy's customer, not Macy's bottom line. You need to do the same. A key element in building relationships is paying more attention to the needs and preferences of your clientele and less on your earnings growth.

Calm down, calm down. Of course, profits are crucial. But

> **Long-term sales success derives from customers who are also there for the long haul.**

And while that department store Santa may lost Macy's a toy sale, he earned them a customer for life.

Step #3 – DON'T FORGET TO WRITE
Relationships have a short shelf life. No matter how charming, enthusiastic or persuasive you are, no one will likely remember you from a business card or a one-time sale. One of the biggest mistakes salespeople make is failing to follow-up immediately after a sale.

If you reach out and make a connection with your customer, the bond between you will be strengthened. Send a 'thank you for your purchase' email and let new customers know you've added them to your **preferred customers list.** This will immediately reinforce who you are, what you do and the connection you've made.

E-mail marketing keeps relationships strong on a shoestring budget. Build your reputation as an expert by giving away some free insight. You have interesting things to say! An easy way to communicate is with a **brief e-mail newsletter** that shows prospects why they should buy from you.

For just pennies per customer, you can distribute an e-mail newsletter that includes tips, advice and short items that entice consumers and leave them wanting more. E-mail marketing is a cost-effective and easy way to stay on customers' minds, build their confidence in your expertise, and retain them.

And it's viral! Contacts and customers who find what you do interesting or valuable will forward your e-mail message or newsletter to other people, just like word of mouth marketing.

Workspace for 3 Action Steps to Superior Relationship Building

Tactical Arena #9 – Superior Brand Building

As we go to press with this book, it's the year 2008...the Year of the Rat according to the Chinese lunar calendar. I think of it as **The Year of the Brand.**

Branding is everywhere – in commerce, in entertainment, in healthcare, and even in politics. Everything is branded today...people, places and things -- from accounting firms and sneakers to presidential candidates and sports drinks.

Seismic Shift

We have moved from a selling world to a buying world. Rather than buying blind and trusting salespeople to guide them, today's consumers want to do their homework and then make a decision. That's why in this day and age..

Good sales require good branding.

'Good marketing' is the process of generating leads. 'Good sales' is the process of convincing prospects, overcoming objections, and getting a check. Both are made easier with good branding. Branding is **influencing and pre-selling**.

Branding appeals to our desires and touches our emotions. Its first goal: to <u>emotionally predispose consumers</u> into entering a business relationship with you. Today, in **The Age of the Individual**, you have to be your own brand. The critical question then is...

What does brand YOU stand for?

The good news is that **branding levels the playing field.** Everyone has a chance to stand out. Everyone has a chance to learn, improve, and show off their expertise...including you.

You, as an individual, are every bit as much a brand as Coca Cola, Virgin Airlines, and Dr. Phil.

To start thinking like your own favorite brand manager, ask yourself the same question the brand managers at Nike, Coke, Pepsi, or the Body Shop ask themselves.

What is it that I do that makes me different?

Your personal brand needs to be

- Compelling to your audience
- Authentic
- Consistent
- Well-known

Forget your job title. Ask yourself: "What do I do that adds remarkable, measurable, distinguished, distinctive value?" Forget your job description. Ask yourself: "What do I do that I am most proud of?"

Take the time to write down your answer. Think of it as a "Give your best answer in 15 words of less" challenge. Let it be a stream-of-consciousness kind of thing. When you're done, take the time to read it and refine it. Several times.

When you're done, you will have created your **brand identity.**

Like it or not, personal branding is unavoidable. As others interact with you, they'll automatically form mental associations that connect you with certain labels, often within the first few seconds: knowledgeable, aggressive, compassionate, cold, etc. It happens automatically because our brains are wired to recognize patterns and form associations.

The labels people attach to you become part of your personal brand.

You can't avoid being labeled, and other people can't avoid labeling you. What you *can* do, however, is control your brand identity by controlling the image you project to the world.

Your external brand is the way you are seen by others. There is an element of choice here. You can decide what to say or write in order to convey a certain image. Your projected image will influence what others think of you and how they might choose to interact with you. You may stumble upon this image accidentally, or you can deliberately target a specific type of image.

Brand takes reputation a step further. Branding means demonstrating and aggressively promoting what you're known for. Essentially, it takes your reputation to a higher level of awareness and publicity.

By branding yourself, you separate yourself from the crowd and create greater impact – for you.

In addition to your external brand, you also have **an internal brand**. This is **what you think of yourself**. Are YOU a brand you feel good about? Is this the same image you project to the world? If you could change your internal brand, what would you change it to? Or, to put it another way:

**Is Brand YOU
something you feel good about?**

When the day is over how do you feel about yourself and the value you have provided? Selling day in and day out can be tough on personal integrity. But truly successful people, both in income and personal self worth stand firm for their beliefs. They communicate their values and do the right thing every day. Do YOU ?

3 Action Steps to Build a Better Brand You NOW

Step #1 – CREATE YOUR BRAND IDENTITY

Your career identity is not some slick piece of advertising. Brand You™ is based on the authentic, talented, and genuinely unique and special person you are. It is not phony or conceited, or an exaggeration, nor is it a trick or fleeting fad.

The components of Brand You are the essence of you as a person, which include: your work strengths, your image, your passion and your personality traits, along with other people's perceptions of you, applied in a work-environment that enhances your productivity.

Before you go any further, you'll need to assemble the key components that will constitute your personal brand. Here are some questions:

- What are your key strengths that will be the foundation of your brand? Knowledge, a network, analytical capabilities, integrity, leadership qualities?

- Who is the target for your brand? What market segment(s) and what constituencies within those companies?

- What value will your potential customer see in your brand? If your customers aren't buying what you are selling, it's all a waste of time.

- What branding have you or your company done previously? Remember, you want your personal brand to complement, not conflict with their brand.

In answering the questions, be honest about who you are -- your attributes and qualities. If you know yourself, you can promote an honest brand. Start by identifying the qualities or characteristics that make you distinctive from your competitors or your colleagues.

What have you done lately -- this week -- to make yourself stand out? What would your colleagues or your customers say is your **greatest and clearest strength**? Your most **noteworthy personal trait?** Don't forget that the way you do things is often as important as what you do.

These factors all influence Brand YOU

Your accomplishments are the foundation of your career brand. Building your brand begins with tracking your **past accomplishments** and *continues* with gaining strategically important **new experiences**. But before you seek out new work, take the time to plan and focus on what you want your brand to stand for -- and develop a strategy for gaining experience in areas of your brand in which you are weak.

So, besides doing your job, ask for new and challenging assignments that will build your brand. Consider **freelancing or consulting**. Use **volunteering** to gain experience.

The more you achieve and accomplish, the brighter your brand will shine – both externally and internally.

Step #2 – CREATE YOUR BRAND STATEMENT
To articulate exactly who and what Brand YOU is, you'll need to create your Personal Brand Statement (PBS). This brief statement expresses in a very compelling way **what you**

have to offer to the world. Your PBS <u>states what you do, your value and what makes you different.</u>

A compelling Personal Brand Statement (PBS) has these characteristics:

- **It's Exciting** - Providing good or excellent service is not enough these days. If you want to create a livelihood from your business (i.e. it's not just a hobby), then you need to stand out from the crowd. Clients are attracted to people who make them go "WOW!"

- **It's Short** - You should be able to say your PBS in one breath. This is like creating a "sound bite" that people can easily remember.

- **It Clearly States The Benefits** - The practical benefit of what you are should be clear or at least clearly implied.

- **It Reflects Your Personality** - Your PBS should be uniquely identifiable with you, and you alone. If any one of your competitors could adopt your PBS, then you need to inject more of YOU™ in it. Your personality can be projected in how you phrase your statement, in the words you use, your tone of voice, etc.

- **It Leaves Them Wanting More -** Your PBS is a "teaser" to start a dialogue with your customer. You're not trying to sell them right then and there.

And of course, you'll want to use that defining statement as often as you can.

- In your email "signature" above your company name

- When someone asks you what you do or what role you play in your company

- When you introduce yourself in a selling situation. (Think about the difference between, "I'm Bob Smith from Widget Coaching Alliance" and, "I'm Bob Smith. I coach companies to win in highly competitive sales environments.")

- In letters you write to customers and prospects.

The ultimate success of a Personal Brand Statement is how well it creates word of mouth. If your PBS meets all of the above requirements, people will **accurately talk about who you are and what you offer**, triggering the attraction forces that work so well in sales.

Change Is Good
Your PBS will evolve over time, reflecting where you are at a specific moment in time.
Ultimately, even the most brilliantly crafted PBS will become stale. But no worries. As soon as you get bored with it, simply change it!

Step #3 – PERFORM REGULAR MAINTENANCE
A brand truly becomes a brand when people know about it. Ways to get the word out about Brand YOU™ include:

- Networking
- Signing up for high-profile projects
- Showcasing your skills in presentations or workshops
- Writing for internal or external publications
- Volunteering for committees or panel discussions at a conference.

Building a brand is one thing...maintaining it is another. Consider taking some or all of these actions to keep Brand YOU thriving:

- **Send your customers and prospects your own monthly e-mail update**. Simple, short and laden with value. A few links to articles. Your brief analysis. Remember, it comes from *you,* not your company. (And don't forget to include your defining statement in your signature.)

- **Don't miss an industry event or association meeting**. That's where you get to promote your personal brand. (And please, have a plan for "working the event.")

- **Attend security and industry analyst events as well if the industry into which you sell has them.** That's where the CFOs and CEOs present and can be approached. (Do your homework! Know who is going to present and when.)

- **Regularly invite two or three different customers to dinner.** A mini-users group meeting will yield amazing information. Be prepared with one or two relevant and hot issues promoting interaction. (Keep the information flowing, not the booze.)

- **Have a customer version of your resume**. Create a 'narrative' bio. Show the value you deliver. Focus the spotlight on Brand YOU!.

Workspace for 3 Action Steps to Superior Brand Building

The 3 Most Important Things You Can Do To Double Your Sales Now and In The Future

Ultimately, the secret to sales success lies in identifying and mastering <u>the techniques that will work for *your* business.</u> There are many strategies you can use and some will be more valuable to you than others. It's important to know the difference between 'good ideas' and 'good ideas that I can put into practice that are right for my product/service and my prospects.'

In general, **all sales improvement efforts fall into three general categories**

- Increasing the <u>number of customers or clients</u>
- Increasing the <u>value of the average transaction</u>
- Increasing the <u>frequency of re-purchases</u>

Most business owners focus too much of their time and money on getting new customers when what they should do is spend more time on maximizing the transaction value and laying the groundwork for a repeat purchase. It's <u>easier and less expensive</u> to sell to an existing customer than a first-time buyer. You don't have to build trust with an existing customer, so there are fewer obstacles that need to be overcome before the deal is sealed.

It's been proven that the efforts and costs required to land a new customer far exceed those associated with selling to an existing customer. That's why you should take advantage of every sales transaction to **increase the amount of the sale**.

Two methods used to achieve this are cross-selling and upselling. In **cross-selling**, you recommend <u>adding related</u>

<u>products or services</u> similar to the one the customer is purchasing.

In **upselling**, you ask customers to make more expensive purchases in place of the original intended purchase. In addition to increasing sales figures, these powerful sales techniques can:

- **Introduce customers to new products or services.**
- **Turn one-time buyers into long-time customers.**
- **Increase the perceived value of a customer's purchase.**

Your goal -- your mission, should you decide to accept it -- is to design systems and programs that surround these three categories of growth strategies.

- **Choose upsell offers that are relevant** to your customer. If your upsell offers are off-base, you'll lose credibility and possibly lose the whole sale. (In other words, don't cross-sell M&M's to prospects purchasing diabetic testing equipment!)

- **Target top customers** for cross-selling and upselling. Their repeated buying habits are indicators for high sales success.

- **Consider the timing** when cross-selling or upselling. The pitch should seem natural in the sales process.

3 Things You Must Do to Double Your Sales NOW...And Forever

Step #1 – ATTRACT MORE CUSTOMERS

Your first step is to select a niche market that you can easily reach and dominate When you have found your niche, develop an **education-based marketing program** that motivates prospects to contact you to learn more about how you can help them.

It's also important to establish a **robust referral program** that can open new channels of growth.

Finally, give your customers the opportunity to "go on record" by giving you **testimonials** about your great product and/or service.

Step #2 – INCREASE THE VALUE OF THE AVERAGE TRANSACTION

Remember that every interaction with a customer is **an opportunity to cross-sell or upsell**, even customer service interactions. Train your CSR reps (and yourself) to transform routine communications into selling opportunities.

Up-sell your customers so that they will spend more money and add on to their purchase. Suggest accessories, follow-up services, and other 'extras' that complement your customer's purchase. (If you sell luxury sports cars, you can upsell luxury add-ons from cashmere lap robes, to driving gloves, to hood ornaments.)

A powerful way to increase the money that comes your way is to **create value-added packages** that would cost more if purchased separately. Using the luxury sports car dealership again, it's common for salespeople to beef up the revenue from a sale with discounted **options packages.**

Value-added packages are extremely common on the Internet. Information products (like this book) are offered with <u>deep discounts</u> for people who buy additional books or products.

Step #3 – INCREASE THE FREQUENCY OF RE-PURCHASES

In an established business, an average customer purchasing pattern develops and (like the average transaction amount) is usually taken for granted and rarely improved upon. That's a mistake.

Sharing news and offers to past and present customers via telephone or mail generally increases their frequency of repurchase and is one more step owners salespeople can easily take to grow increase sales. It's wise to maintain ongoing communications to present compelling offers that are simply irresistible.

Track your customer's usage and buying patterns to s**uggest purchases right *before* they actually need them**. TThis will effectively keep your competition out of the picture entirely.

And be sure to follow-up with customers to see how they're enjoying the benefits of their purchase and to **suggest products or services that would increase their satisfaction.**

What else can you do to open the door for frequent sales? You can...

- **Provide customers with a menu of possible uses** of the products and services the firm has to offer. Restaurant owners say: "If you want to sell the turkey that's in the refrigerator, you had better put turkey in all its various forms on the menu."

- **Get customers to talk about what they are doing,** planning to do or would like to do. In business, talking about what the firm is doing, planning to do, or cannot find someone to do is a favorite pastime.

- **Always talk about the second sale while working on getting the first sale.** Do not expect customers to know there is a second sale without being told.

- **Offer customers some choices of involvement, price, detail, time, etc**. for accomplishing the same thing. When they consider buying a product/service, many firms refrain from buying the bottom or top of the line or service, usually the choose somewhere between the two, thus leaving the door open for add-on sales.

- **Discuss problems customers are having with vendors** as they relate to the products/services your business has to offer.

The $64,000 Question
The road to getting more second sales is paved with action and effort. It's less rocky when you make it a policy to ask every new customer, every current customer, every past custtomer, every current user of a competitor's product or service, and every researched lead or prospect just one question:

What do you need from me?

Give the people what they want...what they need...and you'll never be hurting for sales.

Workspace for The 3 Most Important Things You Can Do Double Your Sales

Conclusion

That's it! You've done it. You've immersed yourself in the secrets of sales. You've walked onto the field of the 9 Tactical Arenas where sales games are won, and you've learned three steps that will lead you to the winner's podium in any contest.

I'd like to offer you my congratulations...and this one last bit of information:

How To Win Friends and Make Sales
Timeless motivational author Dale Carnegie (of "How To Win Friends and Influence People" fame) suggested that the true path to being a successful salesperson, leader, or well-liked individual was not to focus on your desired outcome, but to **put your attention on the other person.**

He posited that there are six ways to get what you want by making people like you:

- Become genuinely interested in other people.
- Smile.
- Remember that a person's name is to that person the sweetest and most important sound in any language.
- Be a good listener. Encourage others to talk about themselves.
- Talk in terms of the other person's interests.
- Make the other person feel important -- and do it sincerely.

Despite the fact that Carnegie was talking about how to persuade people to adopt your point of view, he didn't offer up a manifesto of manipulative sales techniques. What he really presented was **a recipe for making friends.**

Think about the salespeople whom you like best. Chances are you would describe them as "friendly," "nice," and "likable."

When you get on the phone with them, you don't want to hang up. have the ability of making you feel as if their conversation with you is the only thing in the world that matters to them. *And they're not faking it.*

If this approach appeals to you, here's what to do next in Carnegie's own words: "...if you desire to master the principles you are studying in this book, do something about them. Apply these rules at every opportunity. If you don't you will forget them quickly. Only knowledge that is used sticks in your mind."

And only **action breeds success**. If you want to Double Your Sales NOW, it's time to put down this manual and put the theories into action.

Good luck!

Best wishes,

Mary Shanley

Contact Mary

maryshanley@callttc.com

Thanks again and visit www.callttc.com for more information on sales and lead generation.

www.ingramcontent.com/pod-product-compliance
Lightning Source LLC
Chambersburg PA
CBHW050553210326
41521CB00008B/950